Cover image courtesy of Shutterstock.

ISBN 978-1718617919   © Dr Joanna Kujawa

Dr Joanna Kujawa is a passionate author, speaker and scholar. She received a BA and MA from the Pontifical Institute (University of Toronto). After completing her PhD at Monash University she wrote *Jerusalem Diary: Searching for the Tomb and House of Jesus*, which for three years was a bestselling guide to Jerusalem on amazon.com. Her trip to Jerusalem and study of the Gnostic Gospels aroused her interest in Mary Magdalene. Since then, Joanna has been giving talks and workshops around Australia on Mary Magdalene. She is immoderately passionate about her Goddess News blog, which is devoted to the Divine Feminine in all traditions.

This workbook is based on one of her workshops.

ISBN 978-1718617919   © Dr Joanna Kujawa

Contents

Introduction 5
But Why Journaling? 8
Main Points about the Lost Goddess in Most Traditions 14
Main Points about the Gnostics 15
Who is Sophia? 17
Who is Mary Magdalene? 23
Journaling to Manifest the Lost Goddess in Your Life: 28
Secret Gnostic Traditions of Sophia and Mary Magdalene 28
Page 1 of the Journaling Workshop to Manifest the Lost Goddess in Our Lives 29
Page 2 of the Journaling Workshop to Manifest the Lost Goddess in Our Lives 29
Page 3 of the Journaling Workshop to Manifest the Lost Goddess in Our Lives 35
Page 4 of the Journaling Workshop to Manifest the Lost Goddess in Our Lives 35
Page 5 of the Journaling Workshop to Manifest the Lost Goddess in Our Lives 38
Page 6 of the Journaling Workshop to Manifest the Lost Goddess in Our Lives 41
Page 7 of the Journaling Workshop to Manifest the Lost Goddess in Our Lives 44
Page 8 of the Journaling Workshop to Manifest the Lost Goddess in Our Lives 47
Page 9 of the Journaling Workshop to Manifest the Lost Goddess in Our Lives 50

ISBN 978-1718617919   © Dr Joanna Kujawa

Page 10 of the Journaling Workshop to Manifest the Lost Goddess in Our Lives 53

Page 11 of the Journaling Workshop to Manifest the Lost Goddess in Our Lives 56

Page 12 of the Journaling Workshop to Manifest the Lost Goddess in Our Lives 59

Conclusion.. 62

Introduction

This workbook *Journaling to Manifest the Lost Goddess in Your Life: Secret Gnostic Traditions of Sophia and Mary Magdalene* is for all of you, women and men, who either feel 'stuck' in your lives or feel that your potential has not fully manifested itself yet. These feelings can be accompanied by an intuition that there is more to your lives, that there is possibly a different and more fulfilling, more empowering, way of living. Now and then, you may even feel the inklings of some ancient self-knowledge that tells you there is a hidden, buried part of you longing to be rediscovered, re-awakened and made manifest. And you are right! There is a part of you that speaks to you in moments of sudden joy but which very quickly gets silenced by the daily pre-occupation with what is 'important' in life, or at least by what we are told are the important things in life. And just as quickly we forget and re-bury that beautiful dream of ourselves that—Ah! Our soul tells us—would be so beautiful to live!

I have a secret to share with you.

You are not alone with this feeling and this intuition. They are the voice of your deepest Self—and it does not want you to bury it again. It wants you to connect with it, both spiritually and physically. It wants you to make your inner Light and Wisdom shine.

This voice is known in the many spiritual traditions I have studied and has often been repressed by institutionalised and rigid dogmas that limit you or that even tell you that you are 'sinful', that tell you it is good to be fearful and obedient. They are wrong. They want you to forget your Light and your Wisdom.

I call this Light and Wisdom 'the lost Goddess' or the 'lost Divine Feminine', and this is equally important for both women and men, and everyone else, however they describe themselves. In this workshop I am inviting you to rediscover this all-embracing power within you.

There are many traditions that have spoken or speak of the lost Goddess but this time I want to focus on the lost Goddess in the Gnostic tradition.

Who were the Gnostics?

Some believe they were the early Christians, uncorrupted by what later happened to organised Christianity.

Others believe they are much older than that—and the carriers of an ancient wisdom.

They believed in *Gnosis*, the inner knowing, and personified it as Sophia—the Divine Wisdom.

Later, they believed that Mary Magdalene was the personification of that ancient wisdom in Jesus' life.

It is up to you what you believe or don't believe; this workbook is not about belief. It is about uncovering your own inner Gnosis, your own inner Light and Wisdom, or Sophia, and is an invitation to manifest Her in your life.

This workbook consists of two parts

1. Part 1: A brief explanation of who Sophia is (the Inner light and Wisdom within you)
2. Part 2: A practical Journaling Workshop which, with a few simple steps, will help you uncover the Inner Light and Wisdom within you.

This workbook was originally produced as my Journaling Workshop on Lost Gnostic Goddesses for the Carl Jung Society in Australia. Apart from the Gnostic idea of Sophia, I also partially use Joseph Campbell's framework of the hero's journey from his classic work, *The Hero with a Thousand Faces*.

The best way to use this Workbook is to print it out for an easy journaling experience.

Join us on this journey of self-discovery.

With Love,

Dr Joanna Kujawa

But Why Journaling?

To say that we are all complicated beings and that each of us has many parts to our psyche is an understatement – especially when we need to face turning points and difficult changes in our lives.

Let me share something personal with you which, hopefully, will make this clear.

Turning points in life can be very painful and unexpected but are often necessary to make major changes in life – and sometimes in ways that feel like these changes are made without our own volition or even against our own will. But this is not true. Regardless of how challenging they might be, more often than not we create such transformations for our own (higher) good. I can't tell you how many times in my life I have kicked and screamed through a change and felt terribly wronged by it until – sometimes only years later – realising that not only had I created the change but I had wanted it.

It is my experience that the part of us which kicks and screams is usually our frightened self, while the part that creates the necessary change is our Higher Self (for lack of better terminology). Supposedly unwanted and shocking changes usually happen when we, well, have lied to ourselves for too long, stayed in a job or a relationship that was not serving us anymore except, perhaps, helping to keep us surviving. And I do believe that sometimes it is nothing else but our own soul that can knock us out of survival mode, as if telling us, 'You are more. You carry a divine being within. Act like one! It is not just about the mortgage and the bills.' And then our soul mercilessly throws us into the Sea of Existence to teach us how to swim.

It is a tough lesson, I agree, especially when, in this embodiment, we do have so-called financial responsibilities and the material part of ourselves to support.

Yet, in my experience, if a change happens through the promoting of the soul or of Grace, we are not allowed to drown. On the contrary. **We are given another chance to make a better choice.**

Ernest Hemingway said that the best way to start a story is somewhere in the middle, so this is where I will start.

I was in my early 30s, married and working as a teacher in Toronto. I can't even express to you how much I hated my job. I *hated* it! I know this is an ugly word but, sorry, it fits exactly how I felt then. Not that it was a bad job. But it was not for me! I kept the job because I believed that it would save my marriage, that I would finally 'fit in' and have some money after being a postgraduate student for some time. For those same reasons I had also rejected two prestigious scholarships from the University of Toronto to do my PhD. And, of course, I hoped at the time that teaching would allow me the time to write and I would be able to fulfil my dream of being a writer. But most of the time I was too exhausted to write and too unhappy to even dream.

I was living like this because, quite unconsciously, I was trying to be 'good' by society's standards.

One day, my then-husband and I were on a bus to work (that day we were teaching at the same high school). I looked out at the dirty slush of melting snow on the street then at my husband, whom I loved, and knew that I could not do this anymore.

More than that, I was given a vision. And in that vision, he and I were travelling on that bus for the rest of our lives, teaching in a high school, arguing about money, and wondering what life would have been had we made other choices.

That day, I made a choice that this would not happen. But it was not easy. I had always wanted to live in the tropics, so I applied for jobs around the world and eventually got one in Malaysia.

Nothing made sense at the time. Big changes never make rational sense to anyone, not even to us. All I had then, against the 'advice' of friends and the general noise of the world that was telling me I was wrong, was my journaling. Each day, religiously, I filled the pages of my journal, pouring my thoughts out. And slowly this daily ritual became a way of reclaiming myself.

I thought, 'Why the hell am I leaving everything for another teaching job? I want to write.' But the relentless voice within me said, 'Take it,' so I did.

In Malaysia, a year after teaching in a pre-University program, I was headhunted by an Australian University to teach for them, and I ended up completing a PhD with them as well as travelling and living in the tropics, just as I had always dreamed of doing. In Malaysia I also had the best teaching experiences in my life and began writing again: short stories this time, which were later published in *Best Australian Stories* collections.

From there I moved on to Melbourne where I taught at various universities and tertiary institutions and continued to write.

But that is only a small part of the story. There were other challenges, such as finding myself unemployed after finishing my PhD in Melbourne, having no money to pay the rent, living at a kind friend's while desperately applying for jobs, **journaling and meditating** for hours just to keep sane.

Guess what? It all paid off. The journaling and meditation gave me clarity. The temporary unemployment not only taught me compassion but also gave me an opportunity to join two Australian men who had made some discoveries in the Holy Land and who exposed me to the Gnostic Gospels. I managed to convince them to take me along and offered in return to write a book about their discoveries – *The Jerusalem Diary*, my first book. A few months later, I landed a job at a university.

So what does this all mean and what does it have to do with the Goddess?

In all ancient traditions, the Goddess is represented by a spiral, dancing Energy of Life. Call it Shakti, call it Intuition, or Grace. That Goddess is an expression of our lives. She is our Life: complex, spiral and filled with our Destiny. She reminds us that Life is not meant to be lived in a straight line.

She reminds us, as we follow her guidance, to live fully, to explore life and to trust. Yes, trust. It all works out. But we need to be fearless and trusting. We need to listen to our Inner Voice and NOT the deranged voices of the outside world which only want us to repeat the lives of our ancestors. Perhaps these external voices are well meant but they are, nevertheless, fear based. Perhaps someone does not want us to fulfil our Destiny. That is their problem because they do not have the courage to live their own lives to the fullest. Perhaps they can't for some reason. But *we* can.

That is why, I believe, spiritual practice (rather than worship) is so essential for our growth and connection with the Divine – whatever it is – because it allows us to hear this Inner Voice and helps us to block external noise. This is what the fear is – noise from the outside.

One of my writing goddesses, the French writer Colette, once said (I'm paraphrasing here), 'You can live your life thinking what could have been or you can live your life so one day you can say: Ah what a Life it has been!'

The difficult changes are asking us to make this choice. But to make that choice we need to hear that Inner Voice first. And to hear that Inner Voice we need a tool. Although I do believe that meditation is the best way to do this, it is not necessarily the best starting point. Journaling is. So please accept this gift for exploring your Inner Voice unpolluted by the outside noise. *The Gift of Journaling.*

Main Points about the Lost Goddess in Most Traditions

1. There was a powerful, life-giving Goddess at the origin of creation

2. After a long time, organised religious institutions pushed Her way, ridiculed her and called her an 'abomination'

3. Since then we and the world around us have become unbalanced (psychologically, spiritually, physically)

4. There have always been secret traditions (such as those of the Gnostics, Tantrics and others) which preserve the ancient knowledge and stories

5. Since the late 20th century there has been a significant attempt to bring this Goddess back and return balance to our lives.

ISBN 978-1718617919 © Dr Joanna Kujawa

Main Points about the Gnostics

1. The Gnostics were a part of an early spiritual movement claiming to possess the higher teachings of Jesus

2. They had a different interpretation of Jesus' teachings than those which were promoted by the church and institutionalised in the fourth century

3. They believed they possessed Jesus' secret teachings

4. They were persecuted and called heretics

5. Since the 18th century, Gnostic documents have been uncovered in the deserts of Egypt. These include:

    a) The Gospel of Mary Magdalene, discovered in 1896

    b) The Nag Hammadi discoveries in 1945, comprising the *Gospel of Thomas*, the *Gospel of Philip* and other documents

The Gnostics and the Divine Feminine

1. The Gnostics had many representations of the Divine Feminine

2. One of them was Sophia, also known as the 'Wisdom of God', later translated into Latin as *Spiritus Sanctus* or the Holy Spirit, thus losing her feminine aspect (becoming neuter)

3. Mary Magdalene was for them a representation of Sophia in Jesus' life

ISBN 978-1718617919 © Dr Joanna Kujawa

Mary Magdalene

1. She was not a prostitute

2. In fact, she was not considered to be a prostitute until 591 CE, when Pope Gregory I in *Homily 33* confused her with an unnamed woman sinner from *Luke 7*

3. In the *Gospel of Mary Magdalene* she is portrayed as the most trusted disciple of Jesus

4. In the *Gospel of Philip* she is portrayed as his trusted companion

5. In another Gnostic source, *Pistis Sophia*, Mary Magdalene was called 'the woman who knows it All' and who is infused with the Spirit

Who is Sophia?

The topic of **Sophia and the Lost Goddess** is very close to my heart because it deals with the rejection of the feminine in our belief systems. This rejection is dangerous, as it disempowers both women and men.

It is dangerous for women, since they often live lives of disempowerment.

It is dangerous for men because they often live lives of confusion. Both sexes are trapped in rigid and often outdated models of what it means to be a woman or a man.

More importantly, the need to recover the Sophia, the lost Wisdom in our lives, is beyond rigid gender distinctions. This Wisdom brings clarity and authenticity to our lives.

This ancient Wisdom has been repressed for over 1500 years but, as Carl Jung says, nothing can be rejected forever, and what is repressed will eventually come out—both symbolically and literally.

An example of something which has been repressed and buried resurfacing in a literal, physical way is the discovery of the Gnostic documents in Nag Hammadi in 1945 and the Dead Sea Scrolls in 1947. There was also an earlier uncovering of Gnostic documents, such as *the Gospel of Mary Magdalene*, in the 19th century.

All of these discoveries point us toward a less-dogmatised spirituality and, in some cases, the repressed Divine Feminine.

Who is Sophia?

In practical terms Sophia, the Gnostics believed, represents the most valued, most cherished part of ourselves which we have rejected, covered up and buried. She is our lost potential, both human and divine. Without her, we lose our connection with our own lives and we live the inauthentic life of automatons, unconsciously enslaved by external rules, empty materialism and quiet desperation. However, there is a remedy that has been hidden from us. We can remedy ourselves through Gnosis, which equates to the secret knowledge of ourselves buried for so long that we have forgotten we have it.

We can ask ourselves: If Sophia is the place where mind and heart meet, can we see how different this is from cold rationalising? And how can this change our attitudes towards life?

Below are some main points for discussion about Sophia as a background to the Journaling Workshop. However, you can do the Journaling Workshop without reading the introductory material, if you wish. Or you can proceed straight to the Journaling Workshop and come back to the introductory material only when you need to clarify something.

I am so happy to be able to share this workshop with you, and I have no doubt it will help you to uncover your inner potential through keeping a journal, reflecting upon things you write down and then taking the steps that will move your life in more positive directions.

Symbolically speaking, repressed material comes up in our subconscious—in our dreams and day-dreams, in our half-remembered memories. This is not so surprising on an individual level but it is truly magnificent on a collective level—when all of humanity starts to remember something!

And now, in our time, large parts of humanity are seemingly coming to remember the Goddess or some aspects of the Divine which are missing from our lives and which were represented in ancient myths and religions as the Goddess.

We are beginning to awaken to this Goddess and beginning to wonder who she is and where she is. This wondering can start as simple curiosity, a strange blog read in a rush, or a longing.

The mystics of all religions spoke of this longing—the longing for the divine. And now we long for the Goddess, for the lost aspect of the Divine, for the lost aspect in our own personal lives.

We know that something is missing and that the materialistic world in which we live—and which we are told is the only one—does not give us the full story.

This may even mask a very important story in our lives. It is almost as though we wake from a limiting dream and want to spread our wings but are not sure how. Does this sound familiar? Let's look at Sophia in mythical, philosophical and personal terms.

Sophia: In mythical terms

There is one particular story about Sophia which illustrates this feeling in mythical terms. Sophia, also called the Holy Wisdom of God or Divine Wisdom, was known in Christianity as the Holy Spirit (after translation into Latin she ceased being called Sophia and was instead known as *Spiritus Sanctus*) or the aspect of the Wisdom of God. But in this translation something beautiful, something feminine, was lost.

For Gnostics and early Christians she was the bestower of Grace, or in Hindu terms, the bestower of *Shakti*. Indeed, she *is* the Grace, she *is* the Shakti, and the mystics, as well as those initiated into different Sophia/Shakti traditions, know this as an ecstatic union with the Divine, when we perceive the Universe to be as one with us.

In Western religious traditions, the story of Sophia has been told many times, and always as a story of loss. Sophia is represented as the wisdom, the light of God. She descends to Earth to bring knowledge and to bring light, but instead falls into corporeal matter.

She lapses into our earthly concerns and attachments, and either forgets who she is completely or remembers who she is but has no means to return to her previous glory. In some stories she forgets herself and we forget her so much that she is forced to prostitute herself.

She is forced to sell herself for a living—not necessarily literally, but perhaps symbolically. She sells her life for material goods, for material success, and for the trappings of our diminished selves.

There are Gnostic stories of Sophia—under the new name of Helena—who was the partner of Simon the Magician, a charismatic man/saint/alchemist who lived in Jesus' time and met him. Simon is also described in the Bible, although not in very complimentary terms.

Mary Magdalene was considered by some Gnostics to be Jesus' Sophia. In mythical terms, she is always seen as the partner of a sage; she is his wisdom and also often his beautiful and sensual partner.

She is the feminine aspect of his masculine wisdom, as these can never be separate. If they are separated, as they are now, there is no balance in our lives and there is no balance in our world.

In some Gnostic stories the sage eventually grows old, while Sophia stays young and is represented as an ageless woman.

Why? Perhaps Sophia represents our forgotten true selves, our forgotten soul, while the old sage represents the ancient traditions in which the key to reviving our knowledge of Sophia lies.

Sophia: In philosophical terms

Sophia has also resurfaced in all spiritual traditions. In Hinduism, she is called the *Buddhi*—the higher intellect; in Christianity, she is called *Intellection* (a Higher Understanding which allows us to grasp the Truth without rationalising, to understand all at once or at one glance, so to speak).

The Gnostic philosophers called her *Nous*, while modern alternative spiritual traditions refer to her (in a somewhat vague way) as *Intuition*.

Thus, in philosophical terms, Sophia is our ability to see all at once with both mind and heart, OR to see the essence of a given situation which the mind is not capable of grasping. This is a holistic way of seeing. It bypasses any apparent differences and is the ability to see oneness everywhere.

Who is Mary Magdalene?

1. Mary Magdalene is one of the most fascinating and misunderstood women in Western history

Unlike many other Biblical figures, the interest in Mary Magdalene seems to grow rather than fade in the popular imagination.

As a little girl, I spent many punishing hours under my grandmother's tutelage; she hoped to instil in me some religious belief by showing me pictures of Biblical women. Whether right or wrong, she was unsuccessful. I could never relate to any of the scriptural women, the stories of suffering nuns and saints or even the story of the Virgin Mary—no matter how hard I tried.

I resented these women's constant self-sacrifices and martyrdom and the message they were sending out as to how women should conduct themselves. When I grew up I noticed that men, too, were often trapped in a belief about the seemingly mutually exclusive archetypes of the virgin (a good woman) and prostitute (a bad but sexy woman).

I felt that as a woman I could only be one or the other. But once I began to study early medieval history, I was astonished by the richness of material on Mary Magdalene, and I became instantly fascinated. And Mary Magdalene has undergone an interesting evolution, as times and perspectives on the role of women have changed.

2. From the very beginning, Mary Magdalene was considered to be the central figure in the story of the Resurrection

She was the first person to see the resurrected Jesus and the one who brought the news to the rest of the disciples (John 20; Mark 16; Matthew 28). For this reason she was called the 'Apostle of the Apostles' by Saint Augustine, and she is revered in some Gnostic circles as the favoured disciple of Jesus, and called Sophia, the woman 'who knows All'.

3. In at least two Gnostic Gospels, Mary Magdalene is portrayed as Jesus' most beloved and advanced disciple

In the *Gospel of Philip*, for example, Jesus 'kissed her often on her mouth', making the other disciples jealous. In that Gospel she is referred to as Jesus' *koinoinos*, which can mean either a 'wife' or 'companion'.
In the *Gospel of Mary Magdalene*, it is Mary Magdalene who enlightens the other disciples on Jesus' more esoteric teachings, which he has shared only with her. However, in the fourth century during the Council of Nicea (325 CE), both the *Gospel of Mary Magdalene* and the *Gospel of Philip* were rejected as heretical by the Church and were not included in the official version of the Bible. Since then, the importance of her presence in Jesus' life has declined in the popular imagination.

4. She was not thought of as a prostitute until the sixth century

It was not until the sixth century that Pope Gregory I made a scriptural mistake in Homily 33 and confused her with a penitent woman sinner from Luke 7. From that time on **in mainstream Christianity Mary Magdalene has been misconstrued as a prostitute**, even though, in 1969, the Catholic Church admitted Pope Gregory's mistake.

Recently, Catholic scholars have begun changing the story of Mary Magdalene to describe her not as a prostitute but as an older woman of independent means who financially supported Jesus' movement.

5.   Some authors believe she was Jesus' wife…

Margaret Starbird, in her book, *The Woman with the Alabaster Jar: Mary Magdalene and the Holy Grail*, argues that Mary Magdalene is the same person as Mary of Bethany—'the woman with an alabaster jar' who anointed Jesus with 'a very expensive perfume' (Mark 14).

According to Starbird, Mary's family belonged to the once-powerful tribe of Benjamin, and therefore a dynastic marriage between Mary and Jesus (who was said to belong to the tribe of David) was arranged and took place.

By using genealogies from the Old and New Testaments, Starbird concludes that their union was described in the Bible as the wedding at Cana where Jesus turns water into wine.

6. **...And that Mary Magdalene was the Holy Grail**

Starbird argues that Mary Magdalene was, in fact, the Holy Grail, with which medieval troubadours, poets and knights (including the Templars) were so obsessed.

In that version of the story, on the day of the Crucifixion Mary Magdalene, pregnant with Jesus' child, escapes to Alexandria with the help of Joseph of Arimathea. From there, once the baby—a girl called Sarah—is born, they travel on to Southern France.

This is, it is believed, the reason for the worship of Mary Magdalene as the mother of Jesus' child (referred to as *sang raal* or Holy/Royal Blood, rather than *san graal* or the Holy Grail) in Southern France throughout the Middle Ages among the Cathars, a Christian sect that was later considered heretical and purged between 1209 and 1229.

Although Starbird's ideas appear at times farfetched, she has also analysed, apart from Biblical passages, the symbolism of medieval legends, poetry and paintings. And, if some aspects of Mary Magdalene's story were indeed repressed, the author claims that its elements were preserved in the mythical and artistic imagination of the human consciousness.

These are only some of the most well-known, alternative versions of the story of Mary Magdalene. Yet, although the mystery of her 'true' story may never be solved or known, she is the haunting spectre behind Christianity.

She has not only survived an onslaught of historical speculations and papal misinterpretations but has evolved with the times more so than any other figure in western spirituality—and this, in itself, is noteworthy.

More importantly, though, she presents to women a more holistic representation of the feminine as **she crosses the divide between the spiritual and sexual**. She is a mother and an object of sexual desire, a saint and a prostitute, a woman and a favoured disciple in possession of secret knowledge.

Thus, both Sophia and Mary Magdalene symbolise for Gnostics the lost potential within us, the forgotten divinity in our human bodies. Therefore, recovering and manifesting the personal Sophia, the personal Mary Magdalene, in our psyches is also a necessary step to recovering and manifesting them in a broader social, communal life. This recovery and manifestation, both personal and global, will help to bring a lot of balance back to the world. The repressed Divine Feminine aspect of our personal and communal lives needs to be recovered and made manifest to create a better future.

ISBN 978-1718617919   © Dr Joanna Kujawa

Journaling to Manifest the Lost Goddess in Your Life:

Secret Gnostic Traditions of Sophia and Mary Magdalene

A Workbook

By Dr Joanna Kujawa

ISBN 978-1718617919   © Dr Joanna Kujawa

Page 1 of the Journaling Workshop to Manifest the Lost Goddess in Our Lives

For this powerful exercise to succeed, you need to write down your first thoughts without any concern for style or grammar, and especially without any censoring of your thoughts (e.g. do NOT ask yourself: is what I'm writing interesting enough, is it worth writing down, is it okay to write it down?) The point of this exercise is that it is safe and okay to write down everything that spontaneously comes to your mind on this topic, without any censorship.

Now let's begin:

1.   **How do you tell yourself the current story of your life? Is it full of 'buts'? What are some 'buts' in your story and where do they come from? Are they speaking from your soul or from your fear and conditioning?**

_____

_____

_____

_____

_____

_____

_____

_____

_____

ISBN 978-1718617919 © Dr Joanna Kujawa

ISBN 978-1718617919 © Dr Joanna Kujawa

Page 2 of the Journaling Workshop to Manifest the Lost Goddess in Our Lives

Again, Do not censor your thoughts and impressions; just write down what spontaneously comes to mind.

2. What is that long forgotten but still cherished, still lurking dream you have of yourself? Do not say, 'I do not know'— because you do know. Uncover it. Name it. Draw it. Write about this, just for yourself, and do not show it to anyone. This is between you and Sophia: your hidden desire wanting to manifest itself, the inner Sophia, the inner Mary Magdalene, waiting to be uncovered in your life.

_____

_____

_____

_____

_____

_____

_____

_____

_____

_____

_____

ISBN 978-1718617919 © Dr Joanna Kujawa

ISBN 978-1718617919 © Dr Joanna Kujawa

Page 3 of the Journaling Workshop to Manifest the Lost Goddess in Our Lives

Again, do not censor your thoughts and impressions; just write down what spontaneously comes to mind.

Our dreams often express our hidden desires and archetypes. Dreams can be heralds to the Adventure of our Lives, with us as the heroes/heroines at the centre of the Adventure.

3. When was the last time you saw Sophia (the dream)? Could it have been her call to your Adventure, with you as the hero/heroine of your own Life? And if so, when was the last time you thought about this with hope? How did this feel? What thoughts accompany this dream? (If they are thoughts of doubt and discouragement, work through them, because doubts are the liars which kill Sophia.)

_____

_____

_____

_____

_____

_____

_____

_____

_____

ISBN 978-1718617919   © Dr Joanna Kujawa

ISBN 978-1718617919 © Dr Joanna Kujawa

ISBN 978-1718617919   © Dr Joanna Kujawa

Page 4 of the Journaling Workshop to Manifest the Lost Goddess in Our Lives

4. Is there something in this dream/longing that does not serve you anymore? If so, what is it? And what might need updating or improving from its original version?

_____

_____

_____

_____

_____

_____

_____

_____

_____

_____

_____

_____

_____

_____

_____

_____

ISBN 978-1718617919   © Dr Joanna Kujawa

ISBN 978-1718617919 © Dr Joanna Kujawa

ISBN 978-1718617919   © Dr Joanna Kujawa

Page 5 of the Journaling Workshop to Manifest the Lost Goddess in Our Lives

5. How would the story of your life look like if Sophia — the dream of a life fulfilled — was fully included in your current life? What would you feel, think and do?

Write this story of your life, the life that your Sophia, your Inner Knowing, calls you to live. Include all the details that come to your mind.

_____
_____
_____
_____
_____
_____
_____
_____
_____
_____
_____
_____
_____
_____
_____

ISBN 978-1718617919   © Dr Joanna Kujawa

ISBN 978-1718617919   © Dr Joanna Kujawa

Page 6 of the Journaling Workshop to Manifest the Lost Goddess in Our Lives

Again, do not censor your thoughts and impressions; just write down what spontaneously comes to mind.

6. We can either accept or refuse the Call to Adventure. If this workshop is the new Call to Adventure to meet, face and manifest your Sophia, what steps could you take now in your life to answer this Call?

Write down three to seven specific steps you would take if you changed your story to include the manifest Sophia in your life. Then make them. ☐

_____

_____

_____

_____

_____

_____

_____

_____

_____

_____

ISBN 978-1718617919   © Dr Joanna Kujawa

ISBN 978-1718617919 © Dr Joanna Kujawa

ISBN 978-1718617919 © Dr Joanna Kujawa

Page 7 of the Journaling Workshop to Manifest the Lost Goddess in Our Lives

7. If you manifest Sophia in your personal life, how could you positively affect the world around you as well and help move it in a positive direction of Unity, Balance, Truth and Love? Which of these elements would you focus on and why?

Or simply: What would your contribution be?

_____
_____
_____
_____
_____
_____
_____
_____
_____
_____
_____
_____
_____
_____

ISBN 978-1718617919   © Dr Joanna Kujawa

ISBN 978-1718617919 © Dr Joanna Kujawa

ISBN 978-1718617919   © Dr Joanna Kujawa

Page 8 of the Journaling Workshop to Manifest the Lost Goddess in Our Lives

Again, do not censor your thoughts and impressions; just write down what spontaneously comes to mind.

8. What steps could you take today to become closer to your Inner Goddess? (It could be something as simple as a going for a walk on a beach, or to a beautiful café for a cup of coffee(with my *Manifest Your Inner Goddess Journal*). For example, *I am in a café, writing in my Lost Goddess Journal with my café latte next to me. I feel relaxed and confident ...*

_____

_____

_____

_____

_____

_____

_____

_____

_____

_____

ISBN 978-1718617919 © Dr Joanna Kujawa

ISBN 978-1718617919   © Dr Joanna Kujawa

ISBN 978-1718617919 © Dr Joanna Kujawa

Page 9 of the Journaling Workshop to Manifest the Lost Goddess in Our Lives

Again, do not censor your thoughts and impressions; just write down what spontaneously comes to mind.

9. What steps could you take next week to become closer to your Inner Goddess? Describe in detail how you imagine this. Write it down as if it is already true in an affirming way. For example, *I have been doing my Lost Goddess journaling for a week now, each day I ... I am feeling already more in touch with that magnificent part of myself ... This week I would also like to ...*

_____

_____

_____

_____

_____

_____

_____

_____

_____

_____

_____

ISBN 978-1718617919   © Dr Joanna Kujawa

ISBN 978-1718617919 © Dr Joanna Kujawa

ISBN 978-1718617919   © Dr Joanna Kujawa

Page 10 of the Journaling Workshop to Manifest the Lost Goddess in Our Lives

Again, do not censor your thoughts and impressions; just write down what spontaneously comes to mind.

10. What steps could you take in a month's time to become closer to your Inner Goddess? Describe in detail how you imagine this. Write it down as if it is already true in an affirming way.

_____
_____
_____
_____
_____
_____
_____
_____
_____
_____
_____
_____
_____

ISBN 978-1718617919   © Dr Joanna Kujawa

ISBN 978-1718617919 © Dr Joanna Kujawa

Page 11 of the Journaling Workshop to Manifest the Lost Goddess in Our Lives

Again, do not censor your thoughts and impressions; just write down what spontaneously comes to mind.

11. What steps could you take in a year's time to become closer to your Inner Goddess? Describe in detail how you imagine this. Write it down as if it is already true in an affirming way.

_____
_____
_____
_____
_____
_____
_____
_____
_____
_____
_____
_____
_____
_____

ISBN 978-1718617919 © Dr Joanna Kujawa

ISBN 978-1718617919 © Dr Joanna Kujawa

Page 12 of the Journaling Workshop to Manifest the Lost Goddess in Our Lives

Again, do not censor your thoughts and impressions; just write down what spontaneously comes to mind.

12. Where would like to be in three years with your Inner Goddess (your own Sophia) fully manifested? Describe in detail how you imagine this. Write it down as if it is already true in an affirming way. For example, *I am now completely the person I wanted to be all my life. I now ...*

_____

_____

_____

_____

_____

_____

_____

_____

_____

_____

_____

ISBN 978-1718617919   © Dr Joanna Kujawa

ISBN 978-1718617919   © Dr Joanna Kujawa

ISBN 978-1718617919 © Dr Joanna Kujawa

Conclusion

I hope that these exercises in journaling have helped you to recover and will help you to manifest your lost Goddess.

The ancient Gnostic traditions around Sophia and Mary Magdalene help us to see what is truly missing in our lives, and how we can bring this back to life. They empower us so we can impact the world with the beauty, wisdom and sensuality of the Divine Feminine, which has been repressed for too long in our civilisation.

If you would like to stay in touch and/or continue to read and work on the Divine Feminine, please sign up to the Goddess News blog and newsletter at: http://www.joannakujawa.com/goddess-news/

Here are some selected readings on the Divine Feminine, the Gnostics and Mary Magdalene.

> *Goddess News Blog* by Joanna Kujawa
>
> *The Gnostic Gospels* by Elaine Pagels
>
> *The Gospel of Mary Magdalene* by Jean-Yves Leloup
>
> *Looking for Mary Magdalene* by Anna Fedele
>
> *Jung and the Lost Gospels* by Stephen Hoeller
>
> *The Hero with a Thousand Faces* by Joseph Campbell
>
> *Goddesses: Mysteries of the Feminine Divine* by Joseph Campbell
>
> *Voices of Gnosticism* by Miguel Conner
>
> *Rebirth of the Goddess* by Carol B. Christ
>
> *Jerusalem Diary: Searching for the Tomb and House of Jesus*

And there are many more.

With love,

Dr Joanna Kujawa

Made in the USA
Columbia, SC
21 December 2022